SMALL GREAT GESTURES

ART

Francisco Llorca

Illustrated by

Isabel Albertos

Translated by Emma Martinez

SMALL GREAT GESTURES
ART

Art is a language that helps us to express ideas and feelings to both ourselves and with others. Although it has always been a part of life, it appears in different forms, depending on the era and the culture in which it develops.

Not only has the concept of art changed over time, so too have artists. From being considered mere craftsmen to being celebrated as geniuses, and from the preserve of only men to the ever-more visible works of women.

This book aims to bring the history of art closer to young readers. Some artists in this book created art that was unlike anything that had been seen before, others approached daily subjects with a new perspective, turning them into something extraordinary. All of them were brave enough to defy the norms of their day and by doing so, changed history and our way of looking at the world.

FRANCISCO LLORCA

Observe Nature
GIOTTO

Italy, 1305

According to his biographers, even as a child Giotto di Bondone had a gift for painting. They say that his teacher, Cimabue, discovered him when he was just a boy, painting as he watched over his father's sheep. Giotto was so talented that Cimabue invited him to work with him.

In those days, the figures painted on the walls and wooden panels in churches looked stiff and lifeless. But Giotto could paint real life in a different way – he observed nature with a fresh look. The result was that his paintings were much more realistic, his characters looked more human and the spaces in which he painted his stories were more than just decorative.

His style soon became very popular and he was bombarded with commissions, like the one he painted in the chapel of the Scrovegni family, one of the richest families in Italy. The frescoes he painted there are still outstanding for their freshness and the profound emotion portrayed in the faces. Giotto had a decisive influence on the works of artists who came after him, who considered him to be the father of modern painting.

Take a Selfie
CLARA PEETERS

Belgium, 1611

In Clara Peeters' day, women who wanted to be painters had to overcome lots of obstacles. Because of social prejudices, they couldn't attend the same artists' workshops as their male peers. Many of them had to content themselves with painting small things like still lifes (flowers, fruit, household objects ...) or family portraits.

But this did not stop Clara from producing works of great detail and elegance and she became one of the best painters of her day. If you look closely, you will discover a secret hidden in many of her works: she painted her own reflection in metal objects and crystal glasses, just like a selfie. It was like a joke, but it was also a gesture of self-affirmation by an artist who was proud of her work.

Although she did not receive the recognition she deserved in her day because she was a woman, centuries later she became the first female painter the Prado museum dedicated an exhibition to, showing the world what a great artist she was.

Paint on Walls
FRANCISCO DE GOYA

Spain, 1819

At the start of the nineteenth century, Spain was a country of hardship and repression. Some people, including the painter Francisco de Goya, fought for a fairer country. However, many of these people were persecuted and imprisoned on the king and church's orders.

When Goya was older, ill and very tired, he took to his home on the outskirts of Madrid. It was feared he would never paint anything interesting again, but it was here that he started painting directly on the walls, filled with the rage of a younger man and the wisdom of his older years.

The results were images of extraordinary power and darkness, like something out of a nightmare. They are known as his Black Paintings and were nothing like the work of other artists at the time. Although historians cannot agree on the singular meaning of the works, there is no doubt Goya was ahead of his time. Not just because of his modern style but also because even then, he was painting the world we live in today.

Create an Exhibition
GUSTAVE COURBET

France, 1855

By the middle of the nineteenth century, strict rules had been imposed on the world of art which threatened to stifle the creativity of many artists. Those that defended a more lively and free style, who didn't want to paint mythological, religious or battle scenes, had difficulties finding galleries to exhibit their works.

This happened to Gustave Courbet, a French artist who took the world around him as his subject, painting political and social scenes using normal people as his models.

When he presented his works at an official exhibition in 1855, they were all rejected. Instead of giving up, Courbet decided to organise an alternative exhibition. He opened a hall he called The Pavilion of Realism. This gave a name to the style that inspired many artists who came after him, who decided to use their paintbrushes to reflect the reality of the world around them.

Paint What Cannot Be Seen
HILMA AF KLINT

Sweden, 1906

Swedish artist, Hilma af Klint, was one of the first women to receive an artistic education in her country. After graduating from the Royal Swedish Academy of Arts, she made a living painting landscapes and portraits. But Hilma had a secret.

Once a week, she would meet with other artists who formed a group called 'The Five'. Together they would hold séances and practise hypnosis. Hilma decided to use her paintbrushes to illustrate what she saw in these meetings. This meant creating a new artistic style that broke with everything that had come before. Her paintings show circles, ovals and spirals and use colours to evoke the spiritual world, beyond what the eye can see.

Unfortunately, the people around her did not understand these paintings and Hilma decided not to show them. It was only after her death that the world discovered the secret works of this mysterious painter. Today, she is considered to have been a radical innovator and the mother of abstract art.

Be Provocative
MARCEL DUCHAMP

United States of America, 1917

Marcel Duchamp was one of the most provocative artists of the early twentieth century. When he lived in France, he exhibited a bicycle wheel as though it were a work of art. This was not just a joke; Duchamp wanted to surprise his audience rather than just create beautiful works of art, so that people would ask questions.

In 1917, Marcel Duchamp went even further and presented a urinal at a New York exhibition, and ironically called it *Fountain*. It was rejected for being in poor taste. Anyway, how could a plumbing device be considered a work of art? But people did start asking questions, such as 'What is art?', 'What is an original work?' and 'Can anyone become an artist'?

Today, his work is considered to be an example of the subversive power of art and the start of the 'conceptual' arts movement. These artists believe that an idea or concept is just as important to a work of art as the object itself.

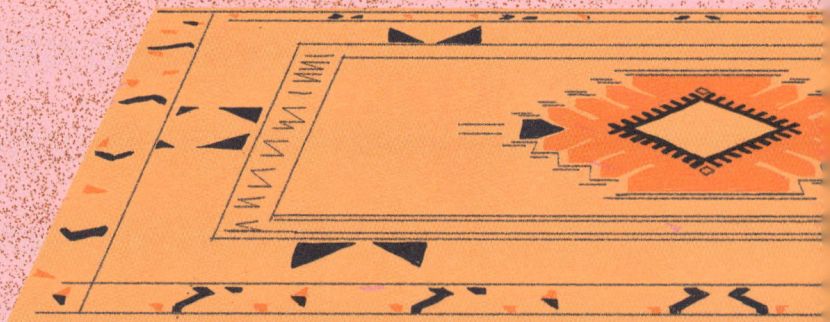

Paint a Self-Portrait
FRIDA KAHLO

Mexico, 1926

Frida Kahlo's life was governed by the consequences of a serious childhood illness and a car accident that left her with injuries all over her body. She had to have several operations and spent long periods in bed, unable to move.

She asked her father for some coloured pencils and paintbrushes to ward off boredom, and her mother had an easel made for her to use lying down. Frida began to study her reflection in the mirror by her bed and transformed her pain into works of art that tell us the stories of important moments in her life and how they made her feel.

But Frida did not only paint herself. She became very involved in the social movements of her era. She spoke against the injustices and problems faced by women in Mexico just because they were women. That is why this ground-breaking woman, who was strong in her opposition to the conventions of her day, is considered not only an artist but a symbol of feminism.

Condemn Violence
PABLO PICASSO

France, 1937

In 1937, Spain was in the midst of a civil war. The Republican government asked Pablo Picasso, the most famous artist of his day, to participate in that year's Universal Exhibition in France, to support their cause. Picasso accepted the offer but for months he was doubtful and could not decide what to paint.

Inspiration arrived on the day he heard of a terrible event. German and Italian bomber planes, under the orders of Nationalists led by General Franco, had destroyed the small village of Guernica and caused a terrible massacre. Picasso shut himself away in his studio looking for an answer to the barbarity and created a violent and moving painting. It depicts an enormous jumble of twisted human and animal bodies, painted in black and white. Today, his *Guernica* is considered by many to be the most important painting of the twentieth century, an icon against the senselessness of war, at any time and in any place.

Disguise Yourself
ANDY WARHOL

United States of America, 1963

Andy Warhol was almost everything an artist can be: painter, film director, writer, publicist, photographer ... you could say there was not just one Warhol, but many.

He was endlessly creative and invented different personas throughout his life. You can see this in his self-portraits and photographs in which he disguised himself, hiding behind a wig and sunglasses or dressed as a woman. For Warhol, life itself could be a work of art.

He was obsessed with fame and the famous. He created an art studio in 1963 called The Factory, which was halfway between being a film set and an art gallery. All the celebrities of the day visited The Factory. Over time, Warhol became a celebrity himself and was convinced that everybody could have their moment of fame, even if it only lasted fifteen minutes. From today's perspective, it seems he was predicting the power of the press, reality shows and social media.

Protest

GUERRILLA GIRLS

United States of America, 1985

In 1985 one of the world's most important museums, the Museum of Modern Art in New York, launched an ambitious exhibition. It was supposed to be a display of the best works in painting and sculpture of the day. However, going through the museum's halls, some people noticed something was wrong. Or rather, that something was missing: of the one hundred and sixty-nine artists represented, only thirteen were women.

Fed up with the way women artists were going unrecognised, a group of women decided to protest. They did this by putting on gorilla masks and demonstrating at the museum's entrance. That was the birth of the Guerrilla Girls. Even to this day, the Guerrilla Girls collective condemn gender inequality in the art world, using ironic and ingenious posters that fill the world's museums and galleries.

Graffiti
BANKSY

England, 2002

A few years ago, some walls in the city of Bristol in England began to appear with strange graffiti. They were interesting and witty drawings made with stencils and aerosols that condemned different kinds of injustice. The works were attributed to a street artist known as 'Banksy', and nobody knew anything about him.

Soon his popularity grew and his works began appearing on walls around the world, drawing attention to different social issues such as the treatment of refugees and freedom of speech. When the streets got too small for him, Banksy started secretly introducing works into museums and collaborating with different non-governmental organisations, music groups and other artists, so that his message would reach more people.

For some he is a vandal, for others he is the leading figure of real street art. One thing is clear about Banksy's work; everybody has an opinion about it.

Observe Nature
Giotto
Italy, 1305

Take a Selfie
Clara Peeters
Belgium, 1611

Paint on Walls
Francisco de Goya
Spain, 1819

Create an Exhibition
Gustave Courbet
France, 1855

Paint What Cannot Be Seen
Hilma af Klint
Sweden, 1906

Be Provocative
Marcel Duchamp
United States of America, 1917

Paint a Self-Portrait
Frida Kahlo
Mexico, 1926

Condemn Violence
Pablo Picasso
France, 1937

Disguise Yourself
Andy Warhol
United States of America, 1963

Protest
Guerrilla Girls
United States of America, 1985

Graffiti
Banksy
England, 2002

© Francisco Llorca, 2020
© Ilustrations: Isabel Albertos, 2020
Graphic Design: Pepe & James; Christina Griffiths

Photographic acknowledgements

Presumed portrait of Giotto, attributed to Paolo Uccello [Public domain] / Wikimedia Commons.

Portait of Clara Peeters [Public domain] / Wikimedia Commons.

Portrait of Goya by Vicent López Portaña [Public domain] / Wikimedia Commons.

Photographic portrait of Gustave Courbet by Nadar [Public domain] / Wikimedia Commons.

Hilma af Klint [Public domain] / Wikimedia Commons.

The French artist Marcel Duchamp © George Grantham Bain Collection (Library of Congress) [Public domain] / Wikimedia Commons.

Frida Kahlo photographed by Guillermo Kahlo in 1932 [Public domain] / Wikimedia Commons Mexico.

Portrait of Pablo Picasso, 1908. Unknown author [Public domain] / Wikimedia Commons.

Andy Warhol at the Moderna Museet in Stockholm before the opening of his retrospective exhibition. Unknown author[Public domain] / Wikimedia Commons.

Guerilla Girls © George Lange (with permission from Guerrilagirls.com).

Banksy artwork known as *Girl with Balloon* or *There is Always Hope*, Great Eastern Street, London.

First published in Spain in 2020 under the title *Pequeños grandes gestos en el arte*
by Alba Editorial, s.l.u.
Baixada de Sant Miquel, 1, 08002 Barcelona
albaeditorial.es

First published in the UK in 2021 by Allison and Busby
11 Wardour Mews
London W1F 8AN
allisonandbusby.com

A CIP catalogue record for this book is available from
the British Library.

ISBN 978-0-7490-2792-6

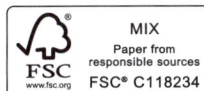

FSC
www.fsc.org

MIX
Paper from
responsible sources
FSC® C118234

Also available

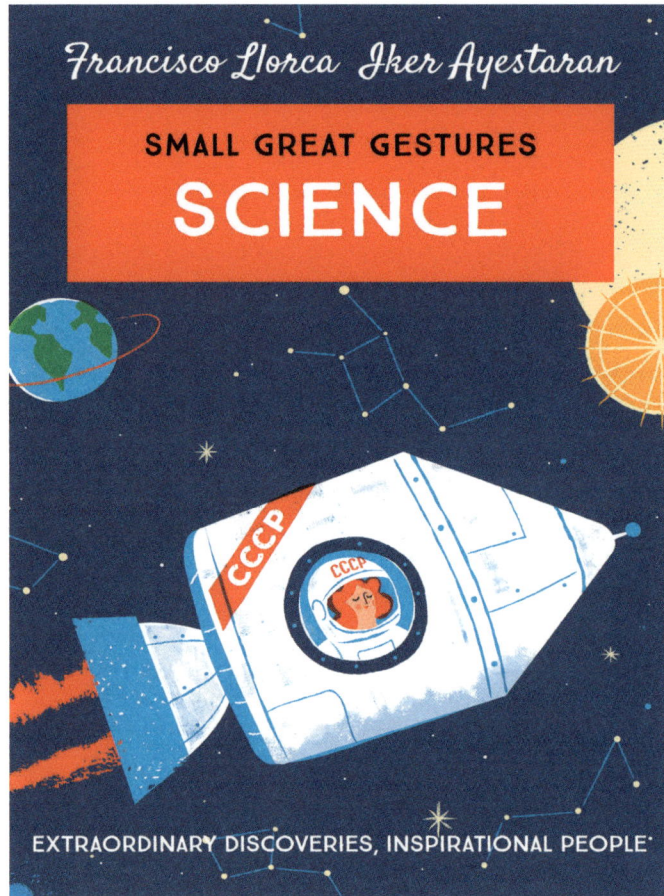

This fun and informative book tells the fascinating stories of remarkable scientists behind ground-breaking discoveries such as penicillin and DNA. From the fall of Newton's apple and Ada Lovelace's imaginative step into the future of computing, to Stephen Hawking's work exploring the origins of the universe, *Science* shows a new generation of scientists that the greatest leaps in understanding start by asking the smallest questions.